January 2022

To all my Peeps on this journey we call life. LIVE! LIVE! LIVE! Take your living seriously. Be intentional about the things you do and engage in. Be intentional about the connections, relationships, and friendship you will create, sustain and nurture. This journey we call life is about you.
Work on you.
Discover you.
Encourage you.
Love you.
Dream for you.
Hold the line for yourself.
Dig for you.
And take this very same love you invested in yourself and then give that to others.

DR.ABC

"Don't search and dig for connections when there is none there - Go live!"
DR.ABC

"Invest quality time looking for love - invest as much in loving yourself too."
DR.ABC

"When you share your ideas, it does not make you have less, it pushes you to stay fresh and current."
DR.ABC

"Bring others with you."
DR.ABC

*"Don't bother to show attitude because you "reach" -
many have reached and turn back.
Stay humble. Play nice."*
DR.ABC

"Learn to wish bitter and bad-minded people the best! No back and forth. Practice it and see."
DR.ABC

"Life is a buffet. Know your taste buds. Let no one force you to eat what you are allergic to. Select and eat only what you desire."
DR.ABC
November 19, 2015

"The only thing you can do with someone who loves you is to love them back."
DR.ABC
March 29, 2016

"Taking a moment of silence for all the persons who are dead on the inside because they allowed others to constantly dictate how they live."
DR. ABC
April 9, 2016

"Live your best life today peeps - we all die."
DR.ABC

"It is very hard to cover a nasty personality with make-up and nice clothes."
DR.ABC
April 12, 2016

"Sometimes you have to let a loser win."
DR.ABC
April 19, 2016

"The best teacher is the constant student. The more I learn the more I realize just how much I don't know."
DR.ABC
May 4, 2016

"Every time you do something for someone you either present, represent, or misrepresent yourself. Do it right. It sticks with you for a long time."
DR.ABC
May 5, 2016

"You must be good from the inside."
DR.ABC
May 9, 2016

"Some of us have perfected the art of tricking others so much that we get up one day and, without even thinking, we have tricked ourselves!"
DR.ABC
May 13, 2016

*"Know yourself first.
Invite others to know you afterwards."*
DR.ABC
May 19, 2016

"Be the kind of friend you want to have."
DR. ABC
May 24, 2016

"Sometimes you get tired of knocking and just kick down the door, and that too is ok. Some doors need to be kicked down."
DR.ABC
June 15, 2016

"Stop asking people who are weaker than you to catch you!!"
DR.ABC
June 20, 2016

"A shark will bite your hook, not because they eat bait, but just to prevent you from fishing."
DR.ABC
June 22, 2016

"Your opponents, distractors, and doubters know when you are winning, they just won't admit it."
DR.ABC
June 23, 2016

"It is good to know your own worth, but it is even better when others are able to recognize and acknowledge that worth."
DR.ABC
June 24, 2016

"Only when some of us are thrown to the wolves, do we discover how much fight and win is in us."
DR.ABC
June 26, 2016

"Never mistake being rude and snobbish for being classy. Classy people are graceful and gracious."
DR.ABC
July 2, 2016

"Stop owing others so much that they own you."
DR.ABC
July 5, 2016

"I hope I never die and leave behind a whole lot of stuff I acquired and forgot to enjoy."
DR.ABC
July 11, 2016

"If, by your own actions, you limit yourself, do not expect others to place value on you."
DR.ABC
July 13, 2016

"In a world that likes photocopy and pretense, it takes effort to be, and remain, original and authentic."
DR..ABC
July 14, 2016

*"You will miss the opportunity to have a great friend
because you listen to the opinion of a bitter enemy."*
DR.ABC
July 20, 2016

"I can understand and possibly accept you being mean to others but, being mean to yourself is dreadful. Be kind to yourself."
DR.ABC
July 24, 2016

"If you tell yourself, you are perfect, then you have given away all your opportunities to grow."
DR.ABC
July 31, 2016

"Think of the last mistake you made. Don't be angry too long. What can you learn from it? Grab that lesson and move on."
DR.ABC
August 2, 2016

"Is it possible that what you did well could be done better?"
DR. ABC
August 3, 2016

"There is a real power in being nice to people who are nasty to you - try it."
DR. ABC
August 4, 2016

"Why do we need to take a flashlight and go looking for love that was professed or promised to us? If it is love, they should let it shine!"
DR.ABC
August 13, 2016

"Do not spend your time hating people who display their gifts and talents so aptly - use that time to find and cultivate yours!"
DR.ABC
August 22, 2016

"There are many good people out there, you just have to accept that some are just not good for you!"
DR.ABC
August 23, 2016

"Not even the queen sleeps in her crown. You got to know when to stop."
DR.ABC
August 28, 2016

"A part of being brave is knowing what you fear."
DR.ABC
August 28, 2016

"Too often we do not know what we need until we need it. Figure out what you need for the journey ahead."
DR.ABC
August 31, 2016

"I want someone to compliment my life, not complicate my life."
DR.ABC
September 2, 2016

"Don't ever get carried away with costumes, masks, magic wands, wishing wells, laser beams, kryptonite, and glitter dust - remain human!"
DR.ABC
September 7, 2016

" We tell ourselves far more lies than we tell others."
DR.ABC
September 10, 2016

"Don't cheat yourself so someone else can win."
DR.ABC
September 11, 2016

"If you are going to be a successful footballer in this game of life, ensure you at least know where the goal posts are located."
DR.ABC
September 18, 2016

"We all get along well with strangers - they know nothing about us. Those close to you must know the real you."
DR.ABC
September 20, 2016

" I will never just accept one slice of bread from anyone, when I know where the bakery is located."
DR.ABC
September 24, 2016

"You can't score any goals if you always volunteer to sit on the bench."
DR. ABC
September 29, 2016

"Stop being so sorry for yourself that you forget you actually can - yes you can."
DR.ABC
September 29, 2016

"Excellence is not magic - it is work."
DR.ABC
October 6, 2016

"We should stop being so surprised when our friends and loved ones are successful and just start being happy, as we had expected them to succeed."
DR.ABC
October 15, 2016

"Don't always trying to do the big things and neglect getting the little things correct."
DR.ABC
October 27, 2016

*"Stop allowing people to treat you badly and
convince yourself it is ok.
It is not ok!!! It is not ok!!!
It is never ok!!!"
DR.ABC
November 4, 2016*

"If people keep hearing your lies, they won't listen to your truths."
DR.ABC
November 12, 2016

"There is certain power in empowering others - try it. The legacy of your leadership should be the growth of your followers."
DR.ABC
December 6, 2016

"Next time you speak to someone, listen to everything they did not say."
DR.ABC
December 6, 2016

*"Because I am good being alone, when I am with company, I can only accept better.
Learn how to be good enough for you."
DR.ABC
December 12, 2016*

"Decide today when is it that you plan to cry your last tear over the same issue."
DR.ABC
February 12, 2017

"Happy people are not constantly mad at the world and everyone! At some point you must let it go."
DR.ABC
March 13, 2017

"Don't be petty - be proactive."
DR.ABC
May 12, 2017

"Water your grass and then point the hose over to your neighbour's grass afterwards."
DR.ABC
May 23, 2017

"What a blessing to own your own thoughts, ideas, and decisions!!!!"
DR. ABC
August 24, 2017

"Your gain is never my loss; therefore, I will always celebrate you."
DR.ABC
October 2, 2017

"I could be nasty or spiteful or malicious or bad-minded or bitter, but that would be like self-destruction - since I know I will reap what I sow!"
DR.ABC
October 11, 2017

"When you help others to shine, you automatically get caught in the reflection."
DR.ABC
October 25, 2017

"Before any act of celebration, there must be some form of accomplishment. Figure out how you will accomplish before you plan how to celebrate."
DR.ABC
May 11, 2017

"Not every 'clap han' is an applause."
DR.ABC
November 11, 2017

"Forgetting your worth is almost as bad as being in a coma - you are left to the mercies of others to care for you."
DR.ABC
November 22, 2017

"They deliberately moved the goal post, but you still scored."
DR.ABC

"Makes no sense you have a crowd around you but not friends."
DR.ABC

"Someone has to hold the light."
DR. ABC
November 9, 2020

"Don't live your life in competition. Live your life in competence. You always win."
DR. ABC

"Put your best living forward. Do not save it all up for a rainy day. It is raining now."
DR. ABC

"Work hard and make all the money, but make sure you are healthy enough to spend it. Self-care is no longer a choice."
Dr. ABC

"Remember to be kind to yourself today!"
DR.ABC

"A lie is cheap and easy to access. The truth is expensive and valuable. Splurge today!"
DR.ABC

"When you don't have the power or courage to face hate in the world or your personal space, send the love - watch how powerful love is."
DR..ABC

"Do not allow anyone to use you to test-run their new emotion."
DR. ABC

"Why are you sitting in hurt and pain waiting for an apology? Apologize to yourself and move on - they already have."
DR.ABC

"Don't let anyone pressure you to save the world - start on your corner."
DR.ABC

"The more you show up as your whole self, the richer your life becomes. Don't make yourself poor."
DR. ABC

"Fixing things in your life is different from managing things. Some days you can fix it, other days you have to just manage it. Both are okay."
DR.ABC

> *"Bring your goods to the market and tricks to the circus."*
> *DR. ABC*

"There are so many black people who just don't have the stamina or the bravery to maintain their blackness in certain spaces."
DR. ABC

*"If I am not invited to the feast, I can live with that.
Just don't try to throw me any bones."*
DR.ABC

"Some of you need to pull up your emotion resume. Remind yourself of your value. Stop allowing people to use you."
DR. ABC

"Don't live in regret about those talents you wish you had. Sharpen and use the ones you do have."
DR.ABC

*"If the work you are doing is about healing- you must be authentic.
Anything less will leave you broken."*
DR.ABC

"Stop thinking that you have nothing to put in a Will - you will roll inna you grave fi see who come claim and bruk fight ova it!"
DR.ABC

"Yes, many of us have legitimate sad stories - don't let that be your only story."
DR. ABC

"My joy is not because I have everything I want. It is because I enjoy whatever I have now."
DR.ABC
#remainthankful
#countyourblessings

"Keep that childhood wide-eyed wonder and amazement about new experiences. It keeps you grounded and thankful."
DR.ABC

"I will always show my vulnerability - but you never knowingly get the chance to use me."
DR.ABC

"Be careful how you advertise your water, and people come to your well and it is empty. Dig deep."
DR. ABC

"Want to know what someone really thinks? Give them real honest permission to share and see what you hear."
DR. ABC

"When it looks like a web. Spins like a web. It is a web. And all involved are spiders. I see you."
DR.ABC

"In all your getting - get people."
DR. ABC

"I store up all the love I get and in times when I don't have enough or need some extra for the shit ahead or I am running low, I go into my reserve."
DR. ABC

*"Dear Lord,
Never grant me a wish I can't handle."*
DR.ABC

Made in the USA
Columbia, SC
10 February 2024

dd821549-65f9-4421-b43d-7ba7c69b0180R01